ABOUT CARDIFF

GRAFFEG

About Cardiff
Published by Graffeg
Radnor Court, 256
Cowbridge Road East,
Cardiff CF5 1GZ Wales UK.

First published in
hardback spring 2003, as
'Cardiff Caerdydd'
ISBN 0-9544334-0-8
revised paperback edition
'About Cardiff' first published
October 2005
© Graffeg 2005
ISBN 0-9544334-2-4

Graffeg are hereby identified
as the authors of this work
in accordance with section
77 of the Copyright, Designs
and Patents Act 1988.

All images © photographers

A CIP Catalogue record for
this book is available from
the British Library.

Designed and produced by
Peter Gill & Associates
www.petergill.com

Printed in Singapore

ABOUT CARDIFF

'A Private View'
sculpture by Kevin Atherton, Cardiff Bay.
Photographer, Andrew Davies

A photographic showcase of
this dynamic young city's heritage,
culture, leisure, sport, shopping and
entertainment, from the Photolibrary
Wales collection.

Foreword by Trevor Fishlock.
Edited by Steve Benbow and
Peter Gill.
Written by David Williams.
Published by Graffeg.

Introduction

Cardiff's tradition is that of a salt water city looking outward to the world, and its modern aspiration is to be ever more wide-eyed, engaged and international. Cardiffians are very keen to fulfil their potential for growth and excellence. There is a real sense of opportunity and of history in the making. And while, of course, there is passionate argument – this is Wales, after all – the emphasis in the grammar is on the future tense.

I like it here. This is a genial city on a human scale, intimate, easy and coherent. One of the enduring pleasures is that it is eminently walkable. Almost all you need is close at hand: shops and traffic-free streets, the busy central market, handsome Victorian arcades, theatres, cinemas and concert venues like St David's Hall where the Cardiff Singer of the World competition has launched many stars.

There are plenty of restaurants, pubs rubbed smooth by time, freshly-minted fashionable bars, and the clubs that pulse with night-time vivacity. University life, too, is anchored in the centre of the city and a powerful generator of youthful rhythm and vigour.

Given all this, the amenity, continuity and a sense of tomorrow, it is no wonder that increasing numbers of young men and women are deciding that this is where they wish to live, work and study. Where once they aimed for London they head in their thousands for Cardiff.

The best way to see the shape of the city is to walk the ridge that rises to the north. There's a tremendous panorama. On your right the lovely Vale of Glamorgan rolls gently to the sea, just part of the city's agreeable hinterland. You can see the salmon-stream Taff winding through Radyr and Llandaff and into the heart of the city, making a final snaking curve into Cardiff Bay. It rambles through broad acres of woods and meadows, past Llandaff Cathedral, Pontcanna Fields and the cricket ground and close to the castle ramparts which rise above the trees. The river and its fields endow Cardiff with a distinctive space and elegance. No city in Britain is greener.

Just below Cardiff Bridge the river forms part of the setting of the Millennium Stadium. This is a structure and achievement daring in scale and conception, to my mind breathtaking but not an intrusion; magnificent, but not dominating. As the temple of Welsh rugby and of all the emotions plaited into the national game, it embodies the legends of the Cardiff Arms Park it replaced and honours history. Yet it demonstrates, too, a determination to adapt and stands as a symbol of the spirit of the city, of what Cardiff can do.

continued over

Photographs left to right
Le Gallois restaurant;
National Museum & Gallery
Wales; Ryan Giggs playing
for Wales; St David's Hotel
and Spa; Student disco;
Cardiff Bay.

For all its splendour the stadium remains a part of the intimacy, linking arms with the city and right in the heart of things, a few steps from the main railway station. It is just a punt from Cardiff's foundation stone, the castle. The Romans built the first walls, the Normans shaped an intimidating medieval fist and, as you can see for yourself, the Victorian barons made it all an opulent entertainment. The castle is an arrow-shot from Cathays Park, the Washington of Wales, the majestic Portland stone statement of the city's Victorian and Edwardian ebullience. Coal money was lavishly invested in the baroque City Hall, the National Museum, University, Law Courts and halls of government and culture, all set among lawns and roses in one of Europe's noblest civic centres. Owain Glyndŵr sacked Cardiff in 1404 but the city was big enough to forgive Wales's warrior prince and his statue reigns in City Hall.

To return to the river, we can see how it draws the whole Cardiff story together. It runs its course at last in the drama of Cardiff Bay, and I say drama because it is such a crucible of visionary ideas and debate. The coal that came down the Taff and its sister valleys made Victorian Cardiff a world capital of energy. Its cosmopolitan and rumbustious docklands grew famous in fact and fiction as Tiger Bay. The aftermath of coal was decline and emptiness but also the opportunity for dynamic regeneration of the docks that were once forested with masts. It is a process.

The midwife-cranes and rising buildings of Cardiff Bay's evolving skyline speak refreshingly, sometimes controversially, of things in the making. It's well worth taking the tour. The Cardiff Barrage, the core of it all, is an engineering bravura, a dam and locks enclosing a 500-acre lake mirroring the new waterfront structures, a soaring hotel, restaurants, exhibitions, craft places and leisure domes. The Welsh Assembly is here, the new political focus of Wales. And the Wales Millennium Centre, a world-class theatre and dance and music house that is home to Welsh National Opera. It accommodates six other cultural companies and is the capital base for Wales's largest youth organisation, Urdd Gobaith Cymru, resonating to the sound of young voices.

The serious point of all this, the big idea, is that Cardiff is the necessary city, integral with Wales, with the power and cultural dimension to engage with Europe and the world, to speak with Wales's distinctive voice. The old Welsh expression 'a fo ben bid bont' suggests that leadership depends on building bridges. Today Cardiff the capital builds bridges into the future; one reason why it's exciting to be here.

Trevor Fishlock

Contents

Map 1
South East Wales

Cardiff is easily accessible by means of excellent transport links. The M4 motorway meanders around the northern edge of the city. Cardiff Central railway station has frequent trains to London, just a couple of hours away, and to the rest of the UK.

Cardiff International Airport is conveniently within reach by road and rail. The numbered dots on the maps give the pages where images of each location may be found. As you explore the delights of Cardiff for yourself, they will help you find the places where the photographers identified highlights of this outstandingly photogenic city. Details of Cardiff's main visitor attractions follow.

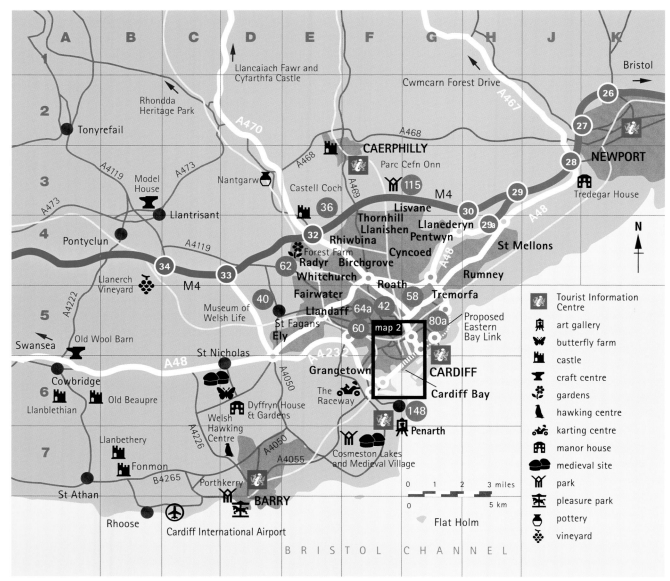

Based upon Ordnance Survey material by permission of Ordnance Survey on behalf of the controller of Her Majesty's Stationery Office.© Crown copyright 100020518

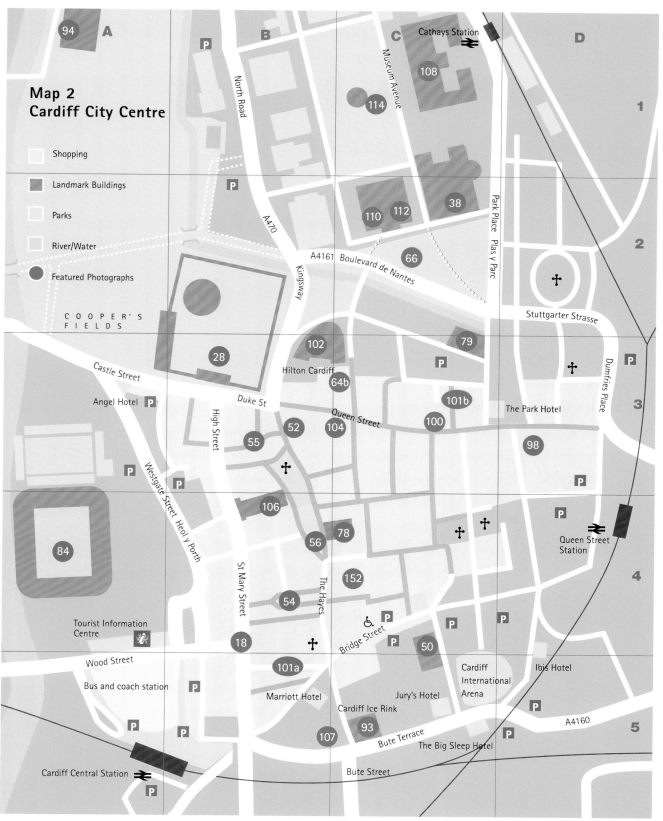

Map 2
Cardiff City Centre

Shopping

Landmark Buildings

Parks

River/Water

Featured Photographs

COOPER'S FIELDS

94

A

North Road

B

A470

Kingsway

A4161 Boulevard de Nantes

C

Museum Avenue

Cathays Station

108

114

110 112 38

66

Park Place Plas y Parc

D

1

2

Stuttgarter Strasse

Dumfries Place

Castle Street

Duke St

Hilton Cardiff

Angel Hotel

High Street

Westgate Street Heol y Porth

28

102

64b

Queen Street

52 104

55

106

79

101b

100

98

The Park Hotel

3

84

St Mary Street

The Hayes

56 78

152

54

18

101a

Marriott Hotel

Tourist Information Centre

Wood Street

Bus and coach station

Cardiff Central Station

Bridge Street

50

107 93

Cardiff Ice Rink

Jury's Hotel

Cardiff International Arena

Bute Terrace

The Big Sleep Hotel

Bute Street

Queen Street Station

Ibis Hotel

A4160

4

5

© The Cardiff Initiative Ltd, based on Aerofilms photography.

11

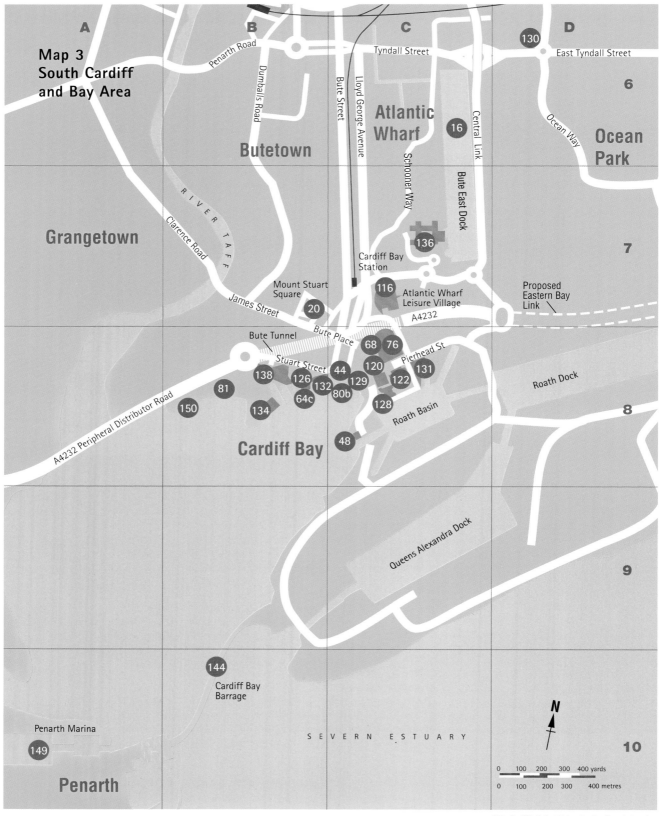

Map 3
South Cardiff
and Bay Area

A B C D

Penarth Road

Dumballs Road

Bute Street

Lloyd George Avenue

Tyndall Street

East Tyndall Street

130

6

Atlantic
Wharf

Schooner Way

Central Link

16

Bute East Dock

Ocean Way

Ocean
Park

Butetown

RIVER TAFF

Clarence Road

Grangetown

James Street

Mount Stuart
Square

20

Cardiff Bay
Station

136

116

Atlantic Wharf
Leisure Village

A4232

7

Proposed
Eastern Bay
Link

Bute Tunnel

Bute Place

Stuart Street

138

81

126

132

64c

44

80b

129

128

68

76

120

Pierhead St

122

131

Roath Dock

A4232 Peripheral Distributor Road

150

134

48

Cardiff Bay

Roath Basin

8

Queens Alexandra Dock

9

144

Cardiff Bay
Barrage

Penarth Marina

149

SEVERN ESTUARY

N

10

0 100 200 300 400 yards

0 100 200 300 400 metres

Penarth

112 City Hall
map 2 ref C2
Cathays Park, Cardiff CF10 3ND
Open: Mon-Fri 8.30am-5.00pm.
Tel: +44 (0)29 2087 1727
www.cardiff.gov.uk/cityhall

28 Cardiff Castle
map 2 ref B3
Castle Street, Cardiff CF10 3RB
Open: every day, all year round, except
Christmas Day, Boxing Day and New Year's
Day. Mar-Oct: 9.30am-6.00pm (last tour/
entry 5.00pm). Nov-Feb: 9.30am-5.00pm
(last tour and last entry 4.00pm).
Tel: +44 (0)29 2087 8100
www.cardiffcastle.com

36 Castle Coch
map 1 ref E3
Castle Hill, Tongwynlais, Cardiff CF15 7JS
Open: Mar-May: 9.30am-5.00pm daily.
Jun-Sep: 9.30am-6.00pm daily.
Oct: 9.30am-5.00pm daily. Nov-Mar:
9.30am-4.00pm Mon-Sat, 11.00am-4.00pm
Sun. Closed for 6 weeks Jan-Feb. Last
admission half an hour before closing.
Tel: +44 (0)29 2081 0101
www.castlexplorer.co.uk/wales/coch/coch.php

42 Llandaff Cathedral
rnap 1 ref F5
Cathedral Road, Cardiff, CF5 2YF
Open for individual visitors 9.00am-6.00pm.
For group visits with a guide, and all other
information Tel: +44 (0)29 2056 4554
www.llandaffcathedral.org.uk

84 Millennium Stadium
map 2 ref A4
Westgate Street, Cardiff CF10 1NS
Open: Mon-Sat first tour 10.00am last tour
5.00pm. Sunday & Bank Holidays first tour
10.00am last tour 4.00pm.
Closed Christmas Day, New Year's Eve,
New Year's Day.
For stadium tours Tel: +44 (0)29 2082 2228
www.millenniumstadium.com

40 Museum of Welsh Life, St Fagans
map 1 ref D5
St. Fagans, Cardiff CF5 6XB
Open: 10.00am-5.00pm daily. Open Bank
Holiday Mondays. Closed Christmas Eve,
Christmas Day, Boxing Day, New Year's Day.
Tel: +44 (0)29 2057 3500
www.nmgw.ac.uk/www.php/mwl/

44 National Assembly exhibition
map 3 ref C8
Pierhead Building, Maritime Road,
Cardiff CF10 4PZ Open: 9.30am-4.30pm
Mon-Fri, 10.30am-6.00pm Sat and Sun.
Tel: +44 (0)29 2089 8200
www.wales.gov.uk/pubinfassematpier/index.htm

38 National Museum and Gallery Wales
map 2 ref C2
Cathays Park, Cardiff CF10 3NP
Open: 10.00am-5.00pm Tue-Sun.
Open Bank Holiday Mondays.
Tel: +44 (0)29 2039 7951
www.nmgw.ac.uk/www.php/nmgc/

79 New Theatre
map 2 ref C3
Park Place, Cardiff, CF10 3LN
Box Office open: 10.00am-8.00pm
Mon-Sat (6.00pm if no evening
performance). Tel: +44 (0)29 2087 8889
www.newtheatrecardiff.co.uk

48 Norwegian Church Arts Centre
map 3 ref C8
Harbour Drive, Cardiff Bay, CF10 5PA
Open: 9.00am-5.00pm daily.
Tel: +44 (0)29 2045 4899
Email: norwegianchurch@talk21.com

58 Scott Memorial Roath Park
map 1 ref G5
Lake Road West, Roath, Cardiff, CF23 5PG
Open: 8.00am-9.00pm daily.
Boating Lake open 11.00am-7.15pm daily
Easter to Sept. Tel: +44 (0)29 2075 5964

138 Techniquest
map 3 ref B8
Stuart Street Cardiff CF10 5BW
Open every day, except for a short
Christmas break. Mon-Fri: 9.30-4.30.
Sat, Sun & Bank Holidays: 10.30-5.00.
Last admission 45 minutes before closing.
Tel: +44 (0)29 2047 5475
www.techniquest.org

68 Wales Millennium Centre
map 3 ref C8
Bute Place, Cardiff, CF10 5AL
Tel: +44 (0)29 2063 6400
For bookings and information, including
tour details Tel: 08700 40 2000
www.wmc.org.uk

k fryers

West Gate

Castell

Shire hall

Ea

The Key

how it all began

Cardiff's story begins with the Romans. They built a bridge over the river and a fort to guard their road between western Wales – where they mined gold – and their regional capital at Venta Silurum near Newport.

The name Cardiff is said to derive from Caerdidi, Fort of Didius – after Aulus Didius, Roman governor of Britain from AD52 to 57. He commanded the campaign against the Silurian people of south-eastern Cambria, who eventually saw the advantages of the Roman way of life. But our capital's name is also consistent with the early-Welsh name Tyf, for the river Taff. This mutated to Caerdyf, fort on the Taff, and is perpetuated in English as Cardiff. The modern Welsh form, Caerdydd, appeared in the 16th century.

After the Romans left, the Angles and Saxons overran much of southern Britain. But Wales remained unconquered and enjoyed something of a golden age as Celtic saints roamed the land and regional kings combined their territories into an emerging Welsh nation.

Soon after the Battle of Hastings, the Normans marched on Wales. William the Conqueror passed by in 1081, on his way to St David's. Robert FitzHamon built his castle on the site of the Roman fort. The monk and historian (and early spin doctor) Geoffrey of Monmouth reinvented the legends of King Arthur, setting some of them in Cardiff - lending his Norman patrons imagined credibility by association with the famous Celtic hero.

John Speed's Map of Cardiff 1610

The Norman settlement evolved into an English town in a strongly Welsh territory. In 1158, William FitzRobert – Earl of Gloucester and Lord of Cardiff and Glamorgan – was captured by Ifor Bach of Senghennydd and kept prisoner until unjustly seized land was returned.

Prince Llywelyn ap Gruffudd united much of Wales, in defiance of Edward I, before being killed in 1282. He found allies in Glamorgan, prompting Gilbert de Clare – the Red Earl, Edward's son-in-law – to build his vast castle at Caerphilly. Welsh revolutionary hero Owain Glyndŵr razed much of Cardiff in 1404 - his rebellion against Henry IV commanded widespread support.

The Acts of Union of 1536 and 1543, by which Henry VIII extended the authority of England over Wales, made Cardiff the county town of a new Glamorganshire, which included Swansea and Gower. But this did not bring prosperity, though Cardiff was recognised in 1559 as one of the three main ports of Wales. In 1581, Elizabeth I granted the town a Royal Charter. In 1608 James I confirmed the charter but Cardiff remained a rather unremarkable place.

The Industrial Revolution changed everything, as the mineral resources of the valleys north of Cardiff – iron ore, coal and limestone – were extracted and smelted to produce iron to feed foundries and factories. From 1794, the Glamorganshire Canal linked Cardiff with the great iron-producing centre of Merthyr Tydfil, some 24 miles away. This waterway – parts of which may still be seen – was paid for by the Guest and Crawshay families, and other iron masters, for whom Cardiff provided the nearest point of export. But the sea lock that connected the canal to the world could only accommodate relatively small craft. Larger sailing vessels had to be loaded out in the bay, a difficult and expensive exercise. The enormous tidal range also meant that the lock was unusable much of the time, as the sea receded a couple of miles across the mudflats.

Bute East Dock, North end, c.1885

Cardiff's first dock – West Bute Dock – opened in 1839. The Second Marquess of Bute, owner of much of Cardiff's land, invested £400,000 in its construction. The dock gate held back enough water for ships to remain afloat when the tide went out. Coal was brought to the quayside in clanking processions of railway trucks – and tipped noisily, but efficiently, into the waiting holds.

The dock proved hugely successful, providing the Bute Estate with a very healthy income from the port dues levied on every ship. More than any other development, it was the building of this first dock that set Cardiff on course to become the world's largest coal-exporting port and, eventually, the city we know today. Mining boomed in the valleys and, by 1850, the West Bute Dock was handling 900,000 tones of coal annually. It became clear that – as trade increased and sailing vessels were gradually eclipsed by ever-larger steamships – it was time to extend the seaport. Cardiff's fortunate geography lent itself to the construction of more docks. The Second Marquess of Bute had passed

away in 1848, when his son was only a year old. But the Bute family's interests were in the safe hands of trusted friends – the splendidly named Onesipherous Tyndell Bruce and James McNabb – who set to work with energy and determination.

The second dock – the Bute East Dock – opened in 1855. The Roath Basin was completed in 1874, followed by the enormous Roath Dock in 1877. Smaller docks and coal jetties were built at Penarth and in the Ely river. The city's expansion during the second half of the 19th century was spectacular.

Much of today's city centre was built during this time. Strict planning regulations imposed by the Bute trustees – and later the Third Marquess – ensured that commercial and public buildings, and housing, were built to a high standard. The 1851 census recorded some 20,000 inhabitants. By 1901, the burgeoning population exceeded 160,000 and the boom town of Cardiff was known as The Chicago of Wales.

St Mary Street c.1910

In October 1905, Edward VII granted Cardiff the status of a city, with the Chief Magistrate accorded the title of Lord Mayor. This confirmed Cardiff's position as the pre-eminent metropolis of Wales. The city's suitably energising motto is 'Deffro, mae'n Ddydd' - 'Awake, it is Day'. The opening of the Queen Alexandra Dock in 1907 — on 320 acres of land reclaimed from the sea — confirmed Cardiff's position as one of the most important ports of the British Empire.

The 20th century saw many businesses and organisations choosing Cardiff as the natural location for their headquarters in Wales. Steelmaking and engineering became established east of the docklands, while service industries, commerce and public bodies employed thousands in the city centre.

In December 1955, Parliament recognised Cardiff as the capital of Wales — a status consolidated in 1958 by the hosting of the Empire Games. The city has since become a familiar presence to the wider population of Wales through the work and influence of its numerous government, educational, cultural and media organisations.

Cardiff expanded steadily throughout the twentieth century, absorbing formerly rural parishes — Llandaff, Ely, Llanishen, Rumney, Pentwyn, Whitchurch, Rhiwbina and others. Local-government reorganisation in 1974 incorporated outer suburbs from St Mellon's in the north-east to St Fagan's in the west, joined by Llanilltern and Pentyrch in 1996.

Today, Cardiff is one of Europe's most dynamic cities, constantly surprising visitors with its grace, space and cosmopolitan buzz. Since the opening of the National Assembly for Wales in 1999, it has become a capital city in the full sense, as a seat of government. It is a great place to visit and the ideal base from which to explore the coast, countryside, culture and heritage of Wales.

Cardiff Coal Exchange Trading Floor in 1912, on its opening after renovation.

Owain Glyndŵr razed Cardiff | Battle of St Fagans | Glamorgan canal link opened

1404 | 1648 | 1794

Images page 22 left to right, statue of Owain Glyndŵr; civil war re-enactment; Glamorgan Canal.

AD45 Romans built a fort on the site of what is now Cardiff Castle

AD445 Cardiff first mentioned in the Welsh Annals, Annates Cambriae

1091 Robert Fitz-Hamon built a wooden castle within Cardiff's Roman fort

1111 Cardiff's first town wall was constructed of wood

1270 Castell Coch's construction is said to have begun this year

1340 The date of Cardiff's oldest existing charter

1404 Owain Glyndŵr burnt Cardiff, rebelling against the fortress town hated by the Welsh

1536 The Acts of Union divided Wales into counties, Cardiff as county town of Glamorganshire

1538 Cardiff's friaries, The Dominican and The Franciscan were dissolved by Henry VIII

1581 Elizabeth I granted Cardiff its first Royal Charter

1608 James I confirmed Cardiff's Royal Charter

1610 First map of Cardiff completed by John Speed

1642–1646 Civil war between King and Parliament – Cardiff captured by Parliamentary troops

1648 Battle of St Fagan's, the last major civil-war battle, Parliament defeating Royalists

1760 River Taff dredged for ships using town quays

1776 The Earl of Bute married into the Herbert family and became
Cardiff Castle Baron

1794 Glamorganshire Canal opened, linking Cardiff and Merthyr Tydfil

1816 Cardiff's first coal was shipped through the Glamorganshire Canal

1826 The Theatre Royal, Cardiff's first purpose-built Theatre, opened

1839 Bute West Dock was opened by its financier, the 2nd Marquess of Bute

1841 The Taff Vale Railway links Cardiff and Merthyr Tydfil

1855 Bute East Dock was built by the 3rd Marquess of Bute, the first trainload of
Rhondda steam coal from Treherbert was distributed among the poor

1861 Cardiff's first public library was opened in the Royal Arcade

1863 The first Cardiff-built steamship 'The Lady Bute' was launched

1868 William Burges and the 3rd Marquess of Bute start remodelling Cardiff Castle

1871 The 3rd Marquess of Bute began rebuilding Castell Coch

1876 Cardiff Rugby Club formed

1877 The Theatre Royal burnt down, Empire Theatre and Grand Theatre opened

1882 Brains Brewery founded

1883 Cardiff University College formed

1884 Cardiff Arms Park opened, and first Rugby international played –
Wales defeated Ireland

Images page 23 left to
right, Cardiff Docks;
3rd Marquess of Bute;
first grandstand Cardiff
Arms Park.

Marconi sends first radio signal across water	City status granted	Captain Scott sails into Cardiff
1897	1905	1910

Images page 24 left to right, Guglielmo Marconi; visit of the Prince Of Wales; 'Terra Nova'.

1886 Cardiff Coal and Shipping Exchange founded

1887 Roath Dock was built by the 3rd Marquess of Bute to assist coal exports

1891 Cardiff Central Market opens

1894 The Bute Estate gives Roath Park to the people of Cardiff

1897 Pierhead building completed

1897 The first radio signals across water were transmitted by Guglielmo Marconi between Lavernock Point and Flat Holm

1898 Cathays Park purchased by Cardiff Council from the Marquess of Bute, for the new Civic Centre

1905 On 21st October, Edward VII granted city status, with Royal recognition bestowed on 28th October

1906 New Theatre opened

1906 The Law Courts, Museum Avenue and City Hall were opened by the 4th Marquess of Bute

1907 Queen Alexandra Dock was opened by Edward VII

1910 Captain Robert Falcon Scott sails the Terra Nova to Cardiff to take on coal for his Antarctic expedition

1910 First football match played at Ninian Park

1913 Cardiff became the largest coal-exporting port in the world – the first £1million business deal is said to have been struck in The Coal Exchange

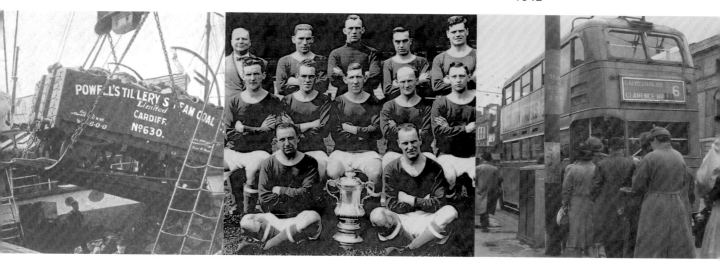

1916 Author Roald Dahl born in Llandaff

1927 National Museum of Wales opened by King George V

1927 Cardiff City won the FA Cup, beating Arsenal – the first time the trophy was taken from England

1928 The War Memorial, commemorating soldiers of the First World War, unveiled by Edward, Prince of Wales

1931 The Welsh National School of Medicine, now the University of Wales College of Medicine founded

1931 Cardiff Airport is opened on Pengam Moors

1941 King George VI and Queen Elizabeth, with Winston Churchill, visited Cardiff following air raids in which many died

1942 The first trolley buses ran and the Glamorganshire Canal carried its last barge

1946 Welsh National Opera formed

1947 John Crichton-Stuart, 5th Marquess of Bute, presented Cardiff Castle and Sophia Gardens to the city

1948 The Welsh Folk Museum opened next to St Fagan's Castle, donated to the National Museum of Wales by the Earl of Plymouth

1950 Castell Coch given to the city by the Bute family

1950 The last shipload of coal left Bute East Dock

1951 Glamorganshire Canal closed

Images page 25 left to right, exporting coal; Cardiff City Football team; Trolley Bus.

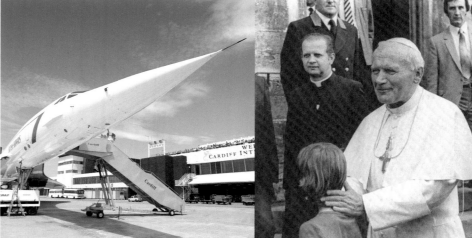

Images page 26 left to right, Cardiff City Coat of Arms; Concorde; Pope John Paul II.

1954 Cardiff/Glamorgan Rhoose Airport opened, along with Cardiff Bus Station

1955 Golden Jubilee of city status

1955 On 20 December, in the House of Commons, the Government recognised Cardiff as the Capital of Wales

1956 26th October was 'Capital Wales Day', permission to augment the coat of arms was granted

1958 Cardiff hosts Empire Games – Wales Empire Pool is built

1964 Bute West Dock closed after almost 150 years of coal shipments

1964 Welsh Office established

1970 Bute East Dock was closed to trade, the last trolley buses were replaced by one-man buses

1971 University Hospital of Wales, the Heath, opened

1973 Sherman Theatre opened

1979 Concorde's first visit to Cardiff

1982 Pope John Paul II visited Cardiff and was made a Freeman

1983 HRH The Queen Mother opened St David's Hall

1986 Wales National Ice Rink opened

1987 Cardiff Bay Development Corporation set up to regenerate the docklands

1988 New County Hall building opened at Atlantic Wharf

Nelson Mandela receives freedom of City	HRH Queen Elizabeth II opens Welsh Assembly	Wales Millennium Centre opens
1998	1999	2004

1989 Leckwith Stadium opened

1991 The Norwegian Church moved to Cardiff Bay waterfront

1994 Construction of Cardiff Bay Barrage began

1995 The new Techniquest building opened – the UK's first purpose-built science centre

1997 The people of Wales voted for a devolved National Assembly

1998 Cardiff hosts the European Union summit

1998 Nelson Mandela receives the Freedom of Cardiff

1999 The first Welsh Assembly was inaugurated by the Queen

1999 The Millennium Stadium opened, Wales hosting the Rugby Union World Cup and defeating the world champions South Africa for the first time

2000 The millennium saw the the completion of the Cardiff Bay Barrage and the regeneration of vast derelict docklands

2001 First FA Cup final at Millennium Stadium

2002 As part of her Golden Jubilee celebrations, the Queen visited Cardiff

2003 Construction of International Sports Village begins

2004 Wales Millennium Centre opened by HRH Queen Elizabeth II

2005 Cardiff celebrates its centenary as a city and fifty years as capital of Wales

Images page 27 left to right, Nelson Mandela; HRH Queen Elizabeth II; Wales Millennium Centre.

2

Cardiff Castle ornate ceiling

Only by visiting Cardiff Castle can you fully appreciate what happened when, in 1866, the third Marquess of Bute – said to be the richest man in the world – commissioned the brilliant but eccentric Victorian architect William Burges to renovate his family home. In designing the extravagant Gothic Revival interior, which conveys the impression of a medieval castle, Burges let his imagination run riot. The almost overwhelming richness of decorative detail – and the outstanding quality of workmanship in every fixture and fitting – will make you smile as the excellent guides lead you from one breathtaking room to another.

heritage

Cardiff is celebrated as one of Europe's youngest capital cities, though its origins and European links date back some 2,000 years. There are important prehistoric sites nearby, but it was the Romans who left us the earliest structure in the city – a walled fort, built in stone.

In medieval times, Cardiff was a modest settlement within the Welsh region of Morgannwg – Glamorgan. The Saxons remained beyond their earthwork, Offa's Dyke, which has largely determined the border between Wales and England ever since.

After 1066, though, the Normans were quick to build a castle in Cardiff and soon conquered much of lowland Wales. But throughout the subsequent centuries of English influence, the treasured Welsh language and culture have survived and evolved.

Cardiff, previously a small fishing port and market town, found its true destiny in the 19th century – with the building of the docks and the rapid boom in coal mining in the valleys to the north.

The need for a seaport to convey vast amounts of coal to the world drew in merchants, agents, clerks, sailors, dockers and railwaymen – along with the many thousands of supporting entrepreneurs and workers who set the scene for the vibrant multicultural city we enjoy today.

Cardiff Castle
south-west towers

Cardiff Castle is a good place to experience a sense of the city's evolution over many centuries. The phases of construction – ancient Roman fort, imposing Norman keep and lavish Victorian showpiece – confirm the strategic advantage and desirability of this prime location on the bank of the River Taff, at the heart of the modern city. Other attractions of Cardiff Castle, which is owned and managed by Cardiff County Council, include the Welch Regiment Museum, traditional Welsh banquets and open-air concerts in the spacious grounds.

Cardiff Castle
The Norman Keep

The Normans advertised and maintained their military might by building a network of stout castles throughout England and lowland Wales. These were typically of motte and bailey design, having a central stronghold on a raised mound, protecting domestic buildings within an encircling earthwork and a ditch or moat. Many towns, including Cardiff, grew from these fortified settlements. The Norman Keep is a substantial stone tower – be sure to make the effort to climb up the steps, to experience panoramic views of the city beyond the castle walls.

Cardiff Castle
Animal Wall

Generations of Cardiff children and city-centre workers have been entertained by the row of animal sculptures along the castle's perimeter wall, between the clock tower and the river. Several of these were given their expressive faces and poses by the sculptor Thomas Nicholls, and date from the 1890s – others were added in the 1930s. This lynx, leaning nonchalantly on the wall, leads a mischievous parade - including monkey, bear, lion, raccoon, hyena and pelican. Those realistic glass eyes seem to be watching the life of the city, and will have seen many changes over more than a century.

Cardiff Castle
Arab Room ceiling

Architect William Burges adopted a different theme – classical, biblical or exotic – for each room. This is the amazing ceiling of the Arab room at the top of the Herbert Tower – an older part of the castle, dating from Tudor times.

The wonderfully detailed marquetry and mosaic work is in Italian marble, of many colours, highlighted with pure gold leaf.

Also distinguished by stained-glass windows of remarkable quality, the room shows how the Marquess of Bute could command the services of the most skilled craftsmen of the day – and provide them with the best materials available – with no expense spared.

Castell Coch

Just north of the city is Castell Coch, named after the 13th-century Red Castle that originally occupied its commanding site overlooking the Taff gorge. The conical towers, nestling in pleasant woodland, make a beguiling sight from the M4 motorway or the A470 just north of Cardiff. Evocative of fairy-tale fantasy or Swiss chateau, this dream palace was designed by William Burges — master of the Victorian Gothic style — as a weekend retreat for the Bute family. The working drawbridge and portcullis lead to an enchanting courtyard and dazzling interiors. The rooms are decorated with beautifully detailed scenes from Aesop's fables — while doors, panels and domed ceilings carry fabulous images and carvings of birds and animals.

National Museum & Gallery, Cathays Park

The elegant exhibition spaces of the National Museum & Gallery are great places to learn about history, art and science. From world-famous works of fine art, including an outstanding collection of Impressionist paintings, to the amazing geology and natural history of Wales; and from the secrets of our Celtic, Roman and Viking ancestors to the newest technology of today; there is a wealth of knowledge, conveyed through fascinating exhibits, waiting to be enjoyed. The museum's curators and educators put on an exciting year-round programme of temporary exhibitions, lunchtime talks, concerts and family activities. And here's a wonderful thing – admission is free!

Museum of Welsh Life
St Fagans

Just west of Cardiff, in one of Europe's most impressive open-air museums, you will find 500 years of history concentrated into 100 acres of beautiful gardens and woodland. The grounds of the Elizabethan manor house of St Fagan's castle contain more than 40 buildings – from 16th-century farmhouse to 1950s pre-fab, from water mill to miners' institute – which have been transported from all corners of Wales and carefully rebuilt. Displays of fascinating items – including farming equipment, rural crafts, household possessions, costumes and musical instruments – illustrate the social history and traditions of Wales. There is a year-round programme of innovative events for all the family. Spring is welcomed, over the May Day holiday, by folk dancers whirling to the stirring sounds of fiddle, harp, crwth and pibgorn – visit the indoor galleries if you'd like to learn about those last two! Gwyl Ifan, a folk-dance festival held in June, attracts participants from other Celtic countries. Horses plough, and food and drink are celebrated, during the Harvest Festival each September. December sees the museum's rescued buildings take on their quaintest air, under lantern light, for the Christmas Tree festival – when mince pies are served and the old chapel comes alive to the sound of traditional carols.

Llandaff Cathedral

The Celtic saints Dyfrig, Teilo and Euddogwy brought Christianity to this ancient sacred site in the 6th century and people have worshipped here ever since. Llandaff's many distinguished bishops include William Morgan, who translated the Bible into Welsh in 1588. The present building is a pleasing blend of Victorian and, following bomb damage in 1941, modern styles. The nave is dominated by Sir Jacob Epstein's glorious statue, Christ in Majesty, installed in 1957. The cathedral precincts are a haven of tranquillity – it is but a short walk from here to the banks of the River Taff, with its impressive weir.

43

Pierhead Building
Cardiff Bay

The broad bay created by the estuaries of the Taff and Ely rivers, and sheltered by Penarth Head, provided an ideal location for a mighty seaport. By 1913, Cardiff was the world's largest coal-exporting centre - with its docks handling some 13 million tons of the vital black diamond. The Pierhead Building, the administrative centre for the docks, is where the ships and their cargoes would be recorded, and port dues levied.

The Pierhead Building is now home to an education centre and an interactive exhibition where you can learn all about the work of the National Assembly for Wales.

Wrth ddŵr a thân

The inscription 'Wrth ddŵr a thân' – 'By fire and water' – underlines the importance of coal in powering the steamships and railway locomotives that transported the raw materials and goods of the Industrial Revolution, and enabled the British Empire to extend its reach throughout the world. South-Wales steam coal was of a very high quality, suitable for use in ships' boilers, and generated relatively little smoke. This made it the favoured choice for the ships of Britain's Royal Navy – their captains could count on an extra margin of safety because a vessel's position would not be betrayed by a column of smoke visible beyond the horizon.

National Assembly visitor centre

The first home of the National Assembly for Wales is nearby, and the new debating chamber just next door. So it seems natural that the Pierhead Building now houses a visitor centre and interactive exhibition where you can learn about the work of the politicians and civil servants who run Wales. The devolved Welsh Assembly Government applies its powers to education, health, transport, local government, culture and economic development – while the UK's security, defence, finances and foreign policy remain the responsibility of Parliament in London.

...essible

...e Assembly

②

Mae'r cyfarfodydd llawn
yn cael eu darlledu'n fyw
ar S4C 2

Plenary sessions are
broadcast live on S4C 2

Gall y Cyhoedd ddod i'r oriel
gyhoeddus i wylio cyfarfodydd
llawn a chyfarfodydd
Pwyllgorau'r Cynulliad

Members of the public can book
to view Assembly meetings (both
plenary sessions and Committee
meetings)

Trosglwyddo Swyddogaethau

Sefydlwyd y Cynulliad ym 1999:

Mai 6
Etholiadau'r Cynulliad
Mai 12
Y cyfarfod llawn cyntaf
Mai 26
Seremoni agoriadol
Gorffennaf 1
Trosglwyddo pwerau'r Ysgrifennydd
Gwladol i lywodraethu Cymru i'r
Cynulliad.

Transfer of powers

The Assembly was established in 1999:

May 6
Assembly elections
May 12
First plenary session
May 26
Opening ceremony
July 1
Powers for the Assembly to govern Wales
were transferred from the Secretary of
State for Wales.

Norwegian Church, built 1868

Cardiff was a familiar port to Norwegian seafarers who crewed ships bringing timber, in the form of pit props, to support the workings of the coal mines of Wales. The Norwegian Church was their spiritual home from home, complete with votive sailing ship hanging from the ceiling.

The author Roald Dahl, whose Norwegian father settled in Cardiff, was christened in this church. The wooden structure was restored and re-opened in its present position on the waterfront as an arts centre in 1992. Nowadays much appreciated as the Norwegian Church Cultural Centre, it is a popular venue for events involving music, literature, poetry and Scandinavian themes – along with exhibitions of paintings and photography. It has a coffee shop that serves good food and has great views of Cardiff Bay.

Scott Memorial, Roath Park lake

In June 1910, Captain Robert Falcon Scott set sail from Cardiff at the start of his last, and ill-fated, expedition to the Antarctic. He had received generous support from the city – including coal for the boilers of his ship, the Terra Nova. He and his crew were given a civic farewell dinner at the Royal Hotel on St Mary Street. Thousands of well wishers watched and cheered as the ship made her way out of the docks and past Penarth Head. This lighthouse-shaped monument in Roath Park lake commemorates Scott and his brave crew – including Welshman Edgar Evans – who reached the South Pole, but tragically lost their lives on their return journey across the ice.

UCG Cinema

There are several multi-screen cinemas in Cardiff, both in the city centre and at Cardiff Bay. The city is regularly chosen for the premieres of feature films made in Wales and is home to three television and radio broadcast companies – BBC Wales, ITV Wales and S4C – and independent film production businesses.
The annual Celtic Film and Television Festival, held in April, is a four-day celebration of film-making talent from Wales, Ireland, Scotland, Cornwall and Brittany. The awards ceremony brings a touch of the Oscars to Cardiff – as do the annual BAFTA Wales presentations, which recognise the endeavours of film and television producers, directors, actors, musicians and technicians.

leisure

Generally acknowledged to be one of the most attractive cities in the UK, Cardiff provides a high quality of life for residents and visitors alike.

The lively city centre has a real buzz – with restaurants, pubs, clubs and cinemas pulling in the crowds. Cardiff is a great place for shopping, ranked in the top 10 in the UK, from the glitz of international brands to the bargains of the excellent Cardiff Market.

The city's famous covered arcades are a delightful echo of Victorian times. Here you will find a treasure trove of chic fashion, books, music, jewellery, Welsh crafts and much else besides. Quaint at any time, they are especially atmospheric when decorated for Christmas.

Generous areas of open parkland and carefully tended public gardens characterise both the city centre and the pleasant suburbs. With the river Taff flowing through the heart of the city, and the foothills of upland Wales providing a backdrop to the north, there is a feeling that nature is close by. The coast, countryside and mountains are within easy reach for those who enjoy a gentle drive or walk, as well as for energetic outdoor pursuits enthusiasts.

The city's prominent sports venues are supported by a network of leisure centres, sports clubs and gyms, and many hotels offer local membership of their health clubs. Whatever your recreational interest, age or fitness level, you are likely to find kindred spirits somewhere in or around Cardiff.

Queen's Arcade

The Queen's Arcade shopping centre is one of several covered malls in Cardiff. Between them, they house many of the leading high-street retailers. Gap, Next, Argos, The Pier and New Look are among the stores to be found in Queen's Arcade, where recent refurbishment has attracted new names. Convenient restaurants and open-air cafés fortify shoppers for their next session of retail therapy. Exciting new developments are happening around the city, with the aim of taking Cardiff's popularity as a superb shopping destination to an even higher level.

Morgan Arcade

Linking St Mary Street and The Hayes, Morgan Arcade is named after the David Morgan department store, which occupied the buildings to either side. After 125 years as a Cardiff landmark, this family-run store closed its doors for the last time in January 2005 – prior to being transformed into smaller shops at ground level and apartments on the upper floors. Between them, Cardiff's arcades house an eclectic range of shops. Check them out for cutting-edge fashion and quirky accessories, high-quality shoes, art and antiques, books, music, stationery and a multitude of distinctive gifts – and enjoy a snack in one of the pleasant cafés.

High Street, Arcade

Of the Victorian shopping arcades that are such a feature of the city, Royal Arcade was the first to be built, in 1858. Castle Arcade – completed in 1887 and found, logically, opposite the castle entrance – is perhaps the most attractive, with its beautiful roof structure. Music shops find a home here, amongst the harmonious architecture. Cardiff Music specialises in classical, jazz and world music, and in the thriving Welsh music scene. On the upper level of Castle Arcade, there is a violin shop and repair workshop much relied upon by the city's orchestras.

Hayes Island, City Centre
With dappled sunlight
filtering through the trees,
and appetising aromas
tempting customers to the
Hayes Island Snack Bar, this
is a pleasant oasis at the
heart of Cardiff's shopping
area. The whole of
The Hayes will be
landscaped, while
preserving its historical
features, as part of the
St David's redevelopment.
Nearby St John's Church has
a handsome tower dating
from the 15th century,
when it would have
dominated the small town.
The Old Library, in the
centre of The Hayes, houses
the Tourist Information
Centre – where the helpful
staff will be happy to
answer your questions
about Cardiff, or anywhere
else in Wales. Other stores
around the Hayes include
Habitat, Waterstones and
the House of Fraser
department store.

Autumn in Roath Park

Cardiff's parks are great places for city dwellers to connect with the ever-changing seasons. The first snowdrops, heralding the end of winter, are followed by springtime's glory of daffodils, summer's riot of blooms and autumn's colourful tapestry.

In April 2005, the Royal Horticultural Society held its three-day Spring Flower Show in Cardiff, as part of the city's centenary events programme. There were floral displays from some of the UK's leading nurseries. RHS experts gave talks and answered questions from keen gardeners.

In celebration of Wales's national flower, they also judged a host of golden entries in the popular 'open daffodil' competition – and a new daffodil variety, named Cardiff, was introduced to mark the city's centenary.

Victoria Park

This much-used open space, off Cowbridge Road East, was opened in 1897 on the occasion of Queen Victoria's Diamond Jubilee. One of Cardiff's most famous residents, Billy the Seal – a female grey seal found in a consignment of fish at Cardiff Docks – lived in the lake from 1912 until 1939. She went exploring when the area was flooded in 1927, but was soon returned to the park – on a tram! When Billy passed away in 1939, her skeleton was placed in the care of the National Museum. She has been immortalised in song by Cardiff's folk-music maestro, Frank Hennessey – and is commemorated by a likeness in Victoria Park, made by sculptor and blacksmith David Petersen.

Roath Park

Take a look at a map of Cardiff and you will see that much of it is green, with an unusually large percentage of the city's area given over to parks and gardens.

Roath Park, with its popular boating lake, is just one of the open spaces that provide breathing space and opportunities for exercise to Cardiff's citizens. Colourful floral displays abound – from the gardens of the Civic Centre to the parks of the outer suburbs.

They reflect the city's commitment to the annual Britain in Bloom competition – which, in return, chose Cardiff to host its awards presentation for 2005.

Radyr Golf Course
There are some 30 golf clubs within a 12-mile radius of Cardiff, many of them having challenging courses in scenic locations. The new Wales National, for example, is one of two championship-standard courses at the Vale of Glamorgan Hotel and Country Club. Wales's golfing credentials are underlined by the selection of The Celtic Manor Resort, Newport – just 20 minutes east of Cardiff – to stage the game's top contest, the Ryder Cup, in 2010. Three other major golfing championships – the Solheim Cup, the Walker Cup and the Curtis Cup – will tee off in south-east Wales before 2010. The Cardiff area made a contribution to golfing history – the Stableford scoring system was devised at the Glamorganshire Golf Club, Penarth, just along the coast from Cardiff.

Le Gallois Restaurant, Cuba café bar, outdoor café Mermaid Quay

As well as being spoilt for choice in the city centre, you will find clusters of restaurants in fashionable Pontcanna and Canton, and around the Inner Harbour of Cardiff Bay. French, Italian, Turkish, Moroccan, Lebanese, Mexican, Indian, Japanese, Chinese and Thai cuisines are among the many represented. The chefs, and their customers, benefit from the tremendous range of high-quality produce available in Wales. The Tides restaurant at the St David's Hotel and Spa is overseen by Marco Pierre White, the youngest chef ever awarded three Michelin stars.

A former colleague of his, Cardiff-born Padrig Jones, presents an enticing modern European menu – including signature Welsh dishes – at Le Gallois in Canton.

Students' Disco
With two universities and a large further-education college, Cardiff is home to more than 25,000 students. Many come from overseas, attracted both by the courses of study and by the quality of life to be enjoyed in this most pleasant of cities. Cardiff University (including the College of Medicine) and the University of Wales Institute Cardiff, are centres of excellence in fields as diverse as engineering, journalism, energy, design, genetics and microelectronics.
Students like to party once in a while – a fair exchange perhaps for the responsibilities many of them will shoulder in future years, when their abilities are put to work in public service or the world of business.

Winter Wonderland

Early in December each year, trucks arrive in front of City Hall and – at the instigation of Cardiff County Council – a magical transformation takes place. A glistening ice rink – surrounded by a funfair, grotto and heated café areas – welcomes faltering beginners and expert skaters to the Winter Wonderland. Cardiff's open-air New Year celebrations and firework display – held around the broad avenues of the Civic Centre – echo the Welsh tradition of Calennig, which marks the passing of the year by the giving of gifts.

3

Wales Millennium Centre
The striking architecture of Cardiff Bay's iconic performance venue, the Wales Millennium Centre, proclaims this landmark building's national significance as a stage for ballet, opera, musical theatre and dance. This powerhouse for the arts also provides offices and a production base for seven of Wales's cultural organisations: Welsh National Opera, Hijinx Theatre, Diversions (the dance company of Wales), Academi (the national literature promotion agency), Touch Trust (providers of creative therapy to adults and children with profound disabilities, including autism), the Tŷ Cerdd music information centre and Urdd Gobaith Cymru, Wales's leading youth organisation.

culture

Cardiff offers a wealth of entertainment, and enrichment for the soul, to audiences in its many performance and exhibition venues.

The city supports orchestras, choirs, theatres, galleries, artists, writers and poets – from enthusiastic amateur activity to the highest professional level. World-class performers appear at the Wales Millennium Centre, St David's Hall, Cardiff International Arena and the New Theatre. The National Museum & Gallery houses collections of international importance and hosts the prestigious Artes Mundi competition every two years. Chapter Arts Centre is a focal point among many smaller beacons of creativity.

Cardiff's distinctive English-language identity gives local writers and poets a potent voice – 'Kairdiff' speech shares words and idioms with other seaport cities. Around one in ten of the population speaks Welsh – Cardiff's Welsh-language community newspaper Y Dinesydd (The Citizen) appeared in 1973, the first of many now published throughout Wales. The Museum of Welsh Life at St Fagan's is the place to learn about the folk traditions of Wales, in both languages.

The famous Welsh enthusiasm for music and literature is conspicuous around the city. Chapels and halls echo to concerts and rehearsals – often in preparation for that most Welsh of cultural events, the eisteddfod. At international level, Cardiff's successes include Welsh National Opera, Shirley Bassey and chart-topping rock bands.

Of course, English and Welsh are but two of the many and varied languages spoken by the people who call Cardiff home, and whose diverse cultures make the city such a fascinating place.

Wales Millennium Centre exterior

The structure is a blend of design and innovative use of materials. Cardiff-based architects Capita Percy Thomas found inspiration in the landscape and industrial heritage of Wales.

A recurring theme of horizontal lines inspired by the sandstone cliffs of the Glamorgan Heritage Coast. Three types of slate lend their rugged character to the front walls.

The distinctive curved roof is made of textured stainless steel, treated to give a pale-bronze patina that reacts to light in extraordinary ways – as variable as the maritime sky over Cardiff Bay. The words above the entrance – windows, in fact – were composed by eminent Welsh poet and writer Gwyneth Lewis. She found the roof reminiscent of smelting furnaces and of the mythical cauldron of Ceridwen, source of inspiration to the medieval Welsh poet Taliesin. 'Creu gwir fel gwydr o ffwrnais awen' means 'Creating truth like glass from inspiration's furnace'. She saw distant horizons in the slate layers – her words 'In these stones horizons sing' evoke the sea, the highway that took coal from Cardiff and brought in many of the city's people.

Wales Millennium Centre interior

The programme of entertainment in the theatres is more than enough reason to visit the Wales Millennium Centre many times a year, but there is yet more to enjoy. Join a behind-the-scenes tour, for an appreciation of the complexity of the building and the work of the companies based here. Or ask about the artsExplorer scheme; a programme of activity that will guide you toward a deeper appreciation of a range of art forms. Look out for free performances in the foyer, pre-show talks and storytelling sessions in the public spaces. A pleasant coffee shop and a stylish restaurant, with an innovative menu, provide the sustenance you will need to enjoy all that the Wales Millennium Centre has to offer.

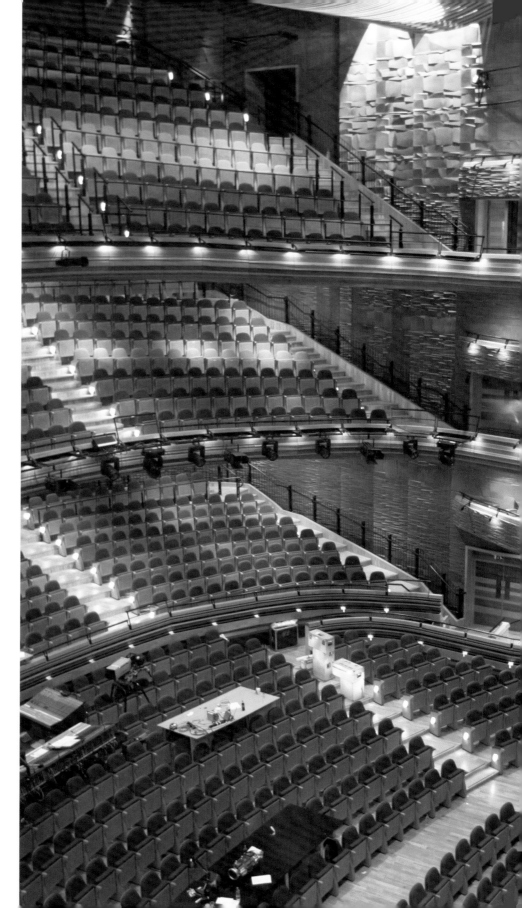

73

Wales Millennium Centre interior

A visit to the Wales Millennium Centre is a real treat for the senses – from your first glimpse of the magnificent building to the satisfying sculptural shapes of the heavy bronze door handles as you go in; and from the beauty of the Welsh hardwoods cladding the balconies and stairs to the joys of a sublime performance onstage. The sumptuous 1,900-seat Donald Gordon Theatre has superb acoustics – adjustable to suit opera and orchestral music, or amplified musical theatre – and excellent sight lines. The 250-seat Studio Theatre provides a platform for interesting new work, enabling talented emerging artists – particularly from Wales – to perform their work.

Welsh National Opera
From modest beginnings some sixty years ago, as an amateur society, Welsh National Opera has grown into the UK's largest touring opera company. As one of the resident arts organisations in the Wales Millennium Centre, it now enjoys a home appropriate to the high musical standards and production values of its gifted singers, orchestral musicians and behind-the-scenes staff. Superb rehearsal rooms, a state-of-the-art stage and advanced technical resources will enable the company to offer an ever-increasing feast of glorious opera.

Welsh Proms at St David's Hall

From the Welsh Proms to world music; from folk singing to heavy rock; from comedians to historical and scientific talks; St David's Hall has it all. This is where you can hear the BBC National Orchestra of Wales, with leading singers and instrumental soloists, and many of the world's orchestras. The prestigious BBC Cardiff Singer of the World competition is held here every two years. A meal in the Celebrity Restaurant, combined with a concert, makes for a most agreeable evening out. There are frequent lunchtime recitals and talks in the informal performance area, Level 3, with jazz concerts, workshops and educational sessions for both children and adults.

New Theatre

This Edwardian playhouse theatre opened in 1906 – just a year after Cardiff gained city status, at the peak of the coal-exporting boom. The opulent interior has welcomed the likes of Laurel and Hardy, Sarah Bernhardt and Anna Pavlova – and was home to Welsh National Opera for more than fifty years.

Nowadays, the popular programme of entertainment includes drama, musicals and pantomime – often featuring household names from television and theatre. The New Theatre is one of several venues that host performances during the Cardiff International Festival of Musical Theatre.

'Secret Station'

As you walk or drive around Cardiff, you will see many striking examples of public art. The tendency during the Edwardian heyday of coal was to put up statues of the city fathers, and the captains of industry and commerce, who made it all happen. Nowadays, the city's pride is expressed in more creative and abstract ways – though often still using industrial materials and themes.

'People like us'

These life-sized figures of a sailor, home from sea, with his girl – and their dog, whose ears have been polished by the attentions of passing children – appeared at an early stage in the bay's development. They have witnessed great progress – from the clearing of the quaysides to the completion of the barrage and the opening of Mermaid Quay. Their real-life counterparts might have lived in nearby Butetown, home to a multicultural community shaped by the history of the seaport. The Butetown History and Arts Centre, a few minutes' walk from Mermaid Quay, tells the story of the old docklands through exhibitions, photographs, life stories, tours and educational programmes.

'A Private View'
Look out for this intriguing
sculpture by Kevin Atherton,
which is situated on the
Butetown Link road from
the M4 to Cardiff Bay,
above the River Taff.
Road access to the
waterfront is excellent but
the aim is eventually to add
walking and cycling access
to the entire 8-mile
perimeter of Cardiff Bay.
There are proposals for a
route from the Inner
Harbour past the Norwegian
Church, new housing
developments and Queen
Alexandra Dock to the
barrage. In the other
direction, the addition of
cycleways over the Taff and
Ely rivers would complete
the circuit via Penarth.

James Dean Bradfield of the Manic Street Preachers
A new generation of Welsh musicians – along with actors in television, theatre and film – has achieved international success in recent years. The novelty of the 'cool Cymru' phenomenon has mellowed into relaxed confidence as Bryn Terfel, Catrin Finch, Ioan Gruffudd, Katherine Jenkins, The Stereophonics, and many others excel yet again. The Manic Street Preachers occupy a special place in the loyalties of Cardiff's rock music fans. They gave a famously fabulous concert in the Millennium Stadium as the closing seconds of 1999 ticked into the new millennium – and performed there again in early 2005, to raise funds for victims of the Asian tsunami.

The Millennium Stadium
Since opening its gates in 1999, to host the Rugby World Cup, the Millennium Stadium has extended a memorable welcome to more than a million visitors each year – to a series of sports events and concerts. Designed to give the best possible views of the action to some 74,000 spectators, this remarkable structure intensifies the sense of occasion that accompanies any great sporting competition. A walkway overlooks the river Taff on one side; the city centre is a very short walk away on the other. The tall masts, and their graceful rigging, convey the weight of the retractable roof to massive anchorages at ground level.

sport

Cardiff is a centre of sporting excellence and home to keenly supported and nationally successful teams in a range of sports including rugby, cricket, football and ice-hockey. The Millennium Stadium, spectacularly located in the heart of the city, is flagship to a wide range of sports venues, large and small.

There are clubs for athletics, basketball, bowls, cycling, golf, hockey, riding, rowing, sailing, squash, swimming, tennis and many other activities. The Wales National Tennis Centre and the National Athletics Centre are both in Cardiff.

The Sports Council for Wales, based at Sophia Gardens, oversees coaching at every level – from children to Olympic hopefuls. Cardiff-born athlete Dame Tanni Grey-Thompson – whose outstanding successes include a record 11 gold medals in Paralympic wheelchair events, from 100m to 800m – is an inspiration to able-bodied and disabled people alike.

Drive northward from Cardiff, for an hour or so, and you will find yourself amid the mountains, lakes and rivers of the Brecon Beacons National Park – perfect terrain for walking, riding, fishing, canoeing, hang-gliding, climbing and caving.

Proximity to the mountain roads and forest tracks of Wales also makes Cardiff a natural choice as headquarters for the Wales Rally GB – the closing round, each autumn, of the World Rally Championship.

Young Welsh rugby supporter

The Millennium Stadium is a family-friendly place and getting there for a major game is straightforward. The stadium sits prominently among the city-centre shops and hotels. It is just a few hundred metres from the railway and bus stations, and within reach from well-signed car parks along the approach roads. The smooth running of the biggest events, including Six Nations games and the FA Cup finals, is testament to the skills of the stadium staff – and to the good humour of the fans as they enjoy the attractions of the city.

For young rugby fans, the autumn series of internationals – against the likes of Fiji, Samoa, the United States, Canada or Japan – provides a great way of seeing their heroes in action.

Millennium Stadium

The Millennium Stadium is built on the site of the legendary Cardiff Arms Park — spiritual home of Welsh rugby for 125 years — and has earned a reputation as one of the world's best sports venues. In addition to rugby (both union and league), it has hosted concerts, religious gatherings, exhibitions, indoor cricket, the British Speedway Grand Prix and soccer fixtures — including, during the building of the new Wembley Stadium, several FA Cup finals. Cardiff is accustomed to welcoming sports fans from all over the world, a tradition endorsed by the inclusion of the Millennium Stadium as a soccer venue in London's bid for the 2012 Olympic Games.

Grand Slam hero
Gavin Henson

In March 2005, a young and talented Welsh rugby team achieved the Grand Slam by beating all other teams in the Six Nations Championship. Thrilling victories over England, Italy, France, Scotland and Ireland gave Welsh people all over the world good reason to be proud. Under the inspired guidance of national coach Mike Ruddock, the team revived the adventurous and entertaining style of play fondly remembered from the great days of the 1970s. They scored 17 tries during the championship, including six in Italy and six in Scotland. The score of 46 points against the Scots was the highest ever, in 118 years as opponents. The victory against England was the first in Cardiff for 12 years. Every member of the team thoroughly earned his share of glory. But one player – Gavin Henson – emerged as a new star when he calmly kicked the crucial match-winning penalty in the closing minutes against England, a moment that the coach has admitted he couldn't watch!

Ryan Giggs in action for Wales

As a multi-purpose, world-class venue, the Millennium Stadium is put to good use by five major sports bodies: The Welsh Rugby Union, The Football Association, The Football League, The Football Association of Wales and the British Speedway Association. In soccer, it has witnessed some great moments – including the FA Cup finals. But most importantly for Welsh fans, it was the scene of their team's celebrated victory over Italy in the Euro 2004 qualifiers. A few weeks before his 18th birthday in 1991, Cardiff-born footballer Ryan Giggs – a long-serving star of Manchester United – became the youngest player ever capped for Wales.

Cardiff Devils ice-hockey team

The speed and skill of the Cardiff Devils ice-hockey team have thrilled their thousands of devoted fans at the Wales National Ice Rink since it opened in 1986. Times are changing though, with the city-centre site set to be redeveloped. The club is currently working with Cardiff County Council toward establishing a secure future at the ice arena due to be built at the Cardiff Bay Sports Village. There are also plans to improve the provision of training, junior hockey and other ice sports. The loyalty of the fans, and the prospect of a new and spectacular home, have made the team – currently riding high in the Elite League – all the more determined to reclaim their rightful place in the sport's Superleague, their natural home for most of their existence.

Cardiff Devils photograph
by Adrian Rapps

Glamorgan County Cricket Club, Sophia Gardens
Founded in 1888, Glamorgan County Cricket Club occupies an idyllic spot on the bank of the river Taff, a five-minute walk from Cardiff Castle. Since 1921, the club has been Wales's representative in the English County Championship, winning it in 1948, 1969 and 1997. Glamorgan has also beaten all of the major cricketing nations – including Australia, who were defeated in 1964 and 1968. Recent years have seen something of a golden era – Glamorgan won the National League in 1993 and 2002. Victory in the one-day league followed in 2004, when the club achieved promotion to Division One of the County Championship.

Powerboat racing

The enclosed waters of Cardiff Bay provide a sheltered and accessible venue for racing under sail and power, with the added advantage of excellent viewing positions for spectators. Powerboats of various classes, including the popular Zapcats – and sailing craft ranging from dinghies to offshore racing yachts – are pushed to the limit as their helmsmen and skippers strive for the smallest advantage. For owners of cruising yachts based in Cardiff, the tidal waters of the Severn estuary and Bristol Channel lead to the scenic coastlines and attractive harbours of Wales, the West Country and Ireland.

Cardiff Marathon, Civic Centre

As a procession of runners heads towards his statue at the end of Queen Street, one can imagine Aneurin Bevan – founder of the National Health Service – smiling contentedly at their fitness and determination. The Cardiff Marathon and Half Marathon are run each autumn. Participants raise substantial funds for more than 150 charities – including the organisers, Barnardo's Cymru. Finishers experience the thrill of emerging from the players' tunnel at the Millennium Stadium, for a lap around the hallowed pitch before crossing the line.

Capitol shopping centre
Queen Street – Cardiff's pedestrianised shopping thoroughfare – is where you will find large branches of W.H.Smith, Boots, Marks and Spencer, Dixon's and other familiar high-street stalwarts. Queen's Arcade, St David's Arcade and the stylish Capitol shopping centre all adjoin Queen Street, and reinforce Cardiff's reputation as one of the top cities in the UK for shopping. Street entertainers enliven the atmosphere – singer Cerys Matthews famously began her career by busking around here.

city

Cardiff is a thriving and forward-looking city having the advantages and resources of a national capital. But its buildings and public spaces have evolved on a manageable scale. The city seems to feel less stressful than many others of similar size. Helpful geography and enlightened planning have produced a pleasant metropolis that never feels too overwhelming.

The generally outgoing character of the city's gregarious people makes Cardiff a noticeably friendly place. The typical citizen will be quick to acknowledge you, and often eager to break into spontaneous conversation.

Most of Cardiff's buildings, roads and bridges came into existence between Victorian times and the present day. The city centre has few medieval or Georgian structures. Firm planning regulations ensure that the distinctive Victorian legacy is conserved as the modern city builds for the 21st century.

The granting of city status in 1905, and promotion to capital of Wales in 1955, have made Cardiff the logical place to establish many of the nation's largest businesses, government bodies and national organisations. The Welsh language is used alongside English in everything from official documents and road signs to shop displays, cash-dispenser screens and till receipts.

The city centre is an enjoyable place to explore, with many fascinating things to see. Even if you have lived here for years, be sure to make time to seek out the unfamiliar.

Queen Street shopping

As befits such a multicultural city, Cardiff offers a range of specialist shops supplying food, clothing, music and crafts from all over the world. In 2004, the city was designated the world's first Fair Trade Capital. Cardiff County Council encourages shops, supermarkets, restaurants, businesses and schools to support products endorsed by the Fair Trade scheme – which gives proper recompense to growers and producers in developing countries.

The council sets a good example by serving Fair Trade tea and coffee in its staff canteens and meetings. The annual Fair Trade fortnight raises awareness of this commendable scheme. Whatever your culinary preferences – meat and two veg, European, Asian, Kosher, Halal, soul food or a nice pot of tea with Welsh cakes – you will find them accommodated somewhere in the city.

Ha! Ha! Café Bar, Greyfriars

Greyfriars is named after the Franciscan friars who settled here in medieval times. Anonymous office buildings have been reinvented as hotels, restaurants and nightclubs, situated within minutes of the city centre's cultural and shopping attractions. The Hilton Cardiff hotel is in the background. The nearby Park Plaza hotel has original Welsh artworks in each of its 129 rooms. There are lively pubs and clubs at the corner of Greyfriars and Park Place, near the New Theatre.

Street dining, Mill Lane

Around Mill Lane, in the city centre, you will find the restaurants and bars of The Café Quarter. Here you may wine and dine al fresco, and watch the world go by. This conversion of a traffic-dominated street into an open-air eating area won the prestigious Street Design Award for Pedestrian Environment. Restaurant owners helped with the planning of one of the most successful groups of street cafés outside continental Europe. Wyndham Arcade, off Mill Lane, is another of the city's architectural treasures.

Hilton Cardiff

This five-star hotel is a remarkable transformation of the former Wales headquarters of Prudential Assurance, built in 1952. It is favoured by visiting stars of stage, screen and sport – and hosts many business events and conferences. The strong steel-framed structure, faced with Portland stone, lent itself to the creation of a new internal layout – including a second-floor swimming pool and health suite – and the addition of the two upper floors. Stylish, top-quality materials, fixtures and fittings – from many countries around the world – are used throughout the interior. The curved shape of the facade reappears as a design motif in corridors, bars and rooms.

Venetian facade

This elegant facade, highlighted by warm afternoon sunshine, brings an evocative touch of Venice to Queen Street. An authentic reconstruction of a Venetian Gothic palazzo, by C.E.Bernard, it would have been all the more convincing in 1870, when it was completed on the bank of the Glamorganshire Canal. This waterway – opened in 1794 and now mostly filled in – gave Cardiff an early start as a seaport. It carried iron from Merthyr Tydfil, for export, in the decades before the coalfield boomed and new railways from the Rhondda, Taff and Cynon valleys converged on Cardiff.

Ashton's fish stall
Cardiff Market

From medieval times until the early-19th century, Cardiff was little more than a modest fishing port and market town serving the agricultural lowlands of Glamorgan. The second Marquess of Bute launched the city into prosperity when, in 1839, he opened the first dock.

The substantial indoor market was built in 1891, as the Victorians gave their busy town centre a fine collection of commercial buildings, many of which remain in use today. Cardiff Market, one of the largest in Wales, is the place to go for fish, meat, vegetables, fruit and an Aladdin's cave of bargains – from clothing to ironmongery; books to pet supplies; crockery to electrical goods.

Brain's pub,
The Golden Cross

The city centre has many buildings of great architectural interest and character. Notable amongst these are the numerous traditional pubs. Samuel Arthur Brain began making his famous beer in 1882, using water from a well under his brewery on St Mary Street. Savouring a pint of Brain's has since become a quintessential Cardiff experience, comparable to enjoying a Guinness in Dublin. The original Brain's site is immortalised as The Brewery Quarter – a development of restaurants, bars and apartments that has received awards for its architectural merit. The characteristic smell of malt and hops, from the modern Brain's brewery on the bank of the Taff, often permeates the air around the city.

Students, Cardiff University

Higher education has long been valued by the people of Wales. Cardiff is a popular centre of learning in many disciplines, from vocational training to advanced research. Cardiff, University has 23 subject departments and more than 1,200 academic and research staff. Cardiff Business School – the largest department, with some 1,800 students – is highly regarded throughout the UK and internationally. The Royal Welsh College of Music and Drama has launched many glittering careers in theatre, film, television and music.

Project Design Research

The first-rate education system is one of the reasons why Wales benefits from an admirable success rate in attracting inward investment. Companies from overseas appreciate the skilled workforce, excellent communications and rewarding quality of life available in Wales.
The emphasis on higher education means that Wales produces a ready supply of graduates and supporting technical staff in today's growth areas of information technology, biotechnology and the service industries. On qualification, many join multinational corporations having a presence in Wales. Others work for specialised home-grown companies or set up in business for themselves.

School children at the Civic Centre

The open spaces in front of the Civic Centre – much enjoyed on fine days by city workers on their lunch break – make it possible to step back and properly take in the splendour of City Hall. The area is a riot of daffodils in spring and colourful floral borders in summer. Gorsedd Gardens, in front of the National Museum, contain a stone circle that commemorates the visits of the National Eisteddfod in 1883, 1899, 1938, 1960 and 1978. A statue of the most distinguished of the UK's Welsh prime ministers, David Lloyd George – in impassioned speechmaking pose – faces the National Museum.

City Hall illuminated

The completion, in 1906, of City Hall, Cardiff's outstanding proclamation of Edwardian civic pride – chimed nicely with the newly granted city status. It provides the centrepiece of the Civic Centre, between the Law Courts and the National Museum and Gallery. The Portland stone frontage and elegant clock tower are richly decorated with Renaissance-style embellishments. The graceful dome is crowned by a suitably intimidating coiled dragon. Pop inside City Hall to see the fine statues of some of Wales's greatest heroes – including St David, Prince Llywelyn and Owain Glyndŵr – and to marvel at the opulent Italian-marble interior.

War Memorial
Cathays Park

Welsh soldiers, sailors and aircrew – both men and women – have given distinguished service in time of war, and continue to do so. The War Memorial – a dignified, classically proportioned structure bearing moving inscriptions in English and Welsh – is at the centre of the immaculately tended Alexandra Gardens, behind City Hall. This is where – on Remembrance Day every November – old soldiers, political leaders and families gather to remember those who made the ultimate sacrifice.

Autumn in Cefn Onn Park

Cardiff's boundaries encompass much more than the urban centre and surrounding suburbs. Country parks, peaceful paths and cycling trails, and even working farmland, are all to be found. Cefn Onn Country Park, located just north of the M4 motorway, is a gem.

In spring, you will find it ablaze with azaleas; in autumn, afire with colour as leaves turn and drop. For a real feeling of being out in the countryside, go for a walk or cycle ride along the lanes and paths rising to the nearby hills of Cefn Cibwr and Coed Y Wenallt – and enjoy fine views over the city to the sparkling sea.

Welsh National Opera performing at Cardiff Bay
The decked arena of Roald Dahl's Plass, originally the entrance basin for Cardiff's first dock, can accommodate audiences of up to 5,000 for open-air concerts. The Pierhead Building lends its distinguished presence, with Queen Alexandra Dock beyond. The Cardiff Bay Barrage is visible between the fireworks and Penarth Head, in the distance. The St David's Hotel and Spa is to the right, beyond the shops and restaurants of Mermaid Quay. A water taxi runs between the Inner Harbour, Penarth and the city centre. If you enjoy getting afloat in something more exciting, there are also speedboat rides – and sailboats may be hired – from the pontoons in front of the Pierhead Building.

bay

The redevelopment of Cardiff Bay — former docklands comprising some 20 per cent of the city's area — is one of Europe's largest and most successful urban regeneration projects.

Following the decline of the coal industry, large areas of quayside and open space — where, over some 150 years, millions of tons of coal were loaded into ships — became available for new uses.

Cardiff's seaport grew around the tidal estuaries of the Taff and Ely rivers, which drained to expose mudflats at low water. The Cardiff Bay Barrage — a landscaped, 1.1km-long sea dam — has transformed the salt-water bay into a 200-hectare fresh-water lake, having a constant water level.

This has created an attractive environment — both visually and in business terms — in which the public and private sectors have combined their efforts to achieve a spectacular transformation. Investment on a vast scale has brought about the development of offices, shops, restaurants, visitor attractions and thousands of new homes. The broad boulevard of Lloyd George Avenue links Cardiff's city centre, only a mile away, to the new waterfront.

The second Marquess of Bute would surely have been pleased that — through his vision in establishing Cardiff's first dock, where the new housing of Atlantic Wharf now stands — he set Cardiff on course toward a glittering future. What a difference a bay makes!

Cardiff Bay aerial

It's always good to have an idea of the layout of a place, so let's go for a tour. The St David's Hotel and Spa is in the foreground on the left, with waterfront apartments just behind. The Techniquest science discovery centre occupies the building with the silver-coloured roof nearby. To the right are the long drydocks where ships were once repaired – the streets of Butetown extend inland. Around the Inner Harbour lie the shops and restaurants of Mermaid Quay, the oval arena of Roald Dahl's Plass, the Pierhead Building, the Wales Millennium Centre and the new National Assembly for Wales debating chamber.

1 Wales Millennium Centre

2 Pierhead Building

3 National Assembly for Wales Debating Chamber

4 National Assembly for Wales

5 Mermaid Quay

6 Harry Ramsden's

7 Techniquest

8 St David's Hotel & Spa

9 Mount Stuart Square

10 UCI Cinema complex

11 Cardiff County Council Building

12 Atlantic Wharf

Illuminated fountains
Cardiff Bay

The public spaces of Cardiff Bay provide a high-quality environment – suitable for everything from major events, attracting thousands of people, to the quiet enjoyment of a walk along the water's edge. Public art is everywhere – ranging from the dazzling Water Tower, in the centre of the picture, to moving reminders of the area's maritime past. Iron pillars bear the names of the mines that sent their coal to Cardiff. John Masefield's evocative poem 'Cargoes' – telling of things, both exotic and mundane, carried by sea – is embossed on a representation of a ship's hatch cover, with sculptures of the cargoes on buildings nearby. Many of the capstans, bollards and iron rings, by which ships were handled in the docks, have been left in place.

The National Assembly for Wales

In a referendum in 1997, the people of Wales voted for a measure of self government, devolved from Parliament. The National Assembly for Wales was opened by the Queen in May 1999. It has 60 elected members: 40 represent constituencies and are elected on a first past the post basis; 20 represent regions and are chosen by proportional representation. The Presiding Officer, who chairs the sessions in the debating chamber, is elected from among the Assembly Members. Debates and committee meetings are bilingual – AMs may use English or Welsh – and simultaneous translation is provided.

Cardiff schoolchildren celebrate at the National Assembly

Cardiff's cosmopolitan nature originates from the mix of incomers attracted, over 150 years and more, to work in the seaport. Many Irish, Italian, Scandinavian, Jewish, Middle-Eastern, West Indian, African and Asian people found a demand for their skills here. Today's communities include descendants of crewmen who worked on ships carrying Welsh coal to their homelands, to fuel passenger and cargo ships voyaging onward to ports in the Americas, the Indian Ocean, the Far East or Australasia. Today, the city's role as capital of Wales – including its worldwide reputation as a centre of learning – continues to attract a healthy influx of new talents and ideas.

New National Assembly for Wales building

Democracy finds a fitting home in the newest landmark building on the waterfront of Cardiff Bay. This innovative structure is designed by the Richard Rogers Partnership and built to the highest environmental standards. The greatest possible use is made of Welsh expertise, products and materials. Steel, slate, wood and glass are prominent in the construction. You will be able to observe the deliberations of the 60 Assembly Members from public galleries overlooking the circular debating chamber, which is illuminated by abundant natural light and designed to create an open atmosphere of co-operation.

Image courtesy of the Richard Rogers Partnership

Mermaid Quay

At the heart of Cardiff Bay is Mermaid Quay, where you will find a fabulous selection of restaurants, cafés and bars. This is the place to indulge in a tempting range of delights from around the world – from traditional Welsh ice cream, to Turkish, Chinese or Thai cuisine, to sushi. Cardiff's first comedy club – The Glee Club – is here. A discount designer shop and an art gallery are nearby.
On summer weekends, especially during the Cardiff Festival months of July and August, the quayside is lined with stalls selling distinctive crafts and gifts.

Atradius Building and Merchant Seafarers' memorial

Atradius, formerly NCM, is the second-largest credit-management company in the world. It was the first large private-sector organisation to move into premises on the waterfront. A staff of 580 is employed in this strikingly angular building between the Pierhead Building and the Norwegian Church.

The nearby Merchant Seafarers' memorial seems at first sight to show the frames and plating of the bow of a ship. You will have to see it for yourself, and walk around it, to appreciate how the sculptor has incorporated a moving representation of the human cost of war at sea.

Landmark sculpture by Pierre Vivant

This imaginative use of road signs marks the approach to Cardiff Bay along a road linking the M4 motorway to industrial east Cardiff, Queen Alexandra Dock and the Inner Harbour. Good road access, clear of the city centre, is part of the planning strategy for Cardiff Bay, benefiting industry, commerce, residents and visitors alike. Tourism road signs, on a brown background, identify another access road from the M4, just west of Cardiff, to the Penarth side of Cardiff Bay.

Scott Harbour Building

The architects of the new buildings around Cardiff Bay were charged with the task of giving the area a vibrant, go-ahead identity that would appeal to an appropriate range of businesses – from multinational corporations to smaller professional firms. The quality and attractiveness of the chosen designs, and the materials used, reflect well both upon the city and on the organisations that base themselves here. Big names in the financial, property, legal, construction and leisure sectors have seen the wisdom of moving into the high-quality premises of Cardiff Bay.

Celtic Ring sculpture
This impressive bronze sculpture takes the shape of a Celtic torq – the neck ring worn, typically in gold, by Celtic chieftains and princesses, and in iron by warriors. It marks the beginning of the Taff Trail – the scenic, long-distance footpath and cycle route that runs from Cardiff to Brecon. The accessibility of numerous railway stations en route means that the trail can easily be tackled in manageable sections. The Cardiff Bay Barrage is in the distance – with its locks and bascule bridges to the right, in the shadow of Penarth Head.

St David's Hotel and Spa
Cardiff's original five-star hotel has 132 rooms, all of which have balconies providing tremendous views of either the Inner Harbour or the wide sweep of Cardiff Bay toward Penarth.

The rooftop feature has been compared to a sail, a bird, a fish and an ocean wave. Whatever you make of it, this building is a fitting landmark for the shoreline of Cardiff Bay. In summer, the hotel's

Tides Restaurant offers al fresco dining on its elevated terrace overlooking the waters of the bay – with water taxis and yachts gliding by below.

Cardiff Council Headquarters

In local-government terminology, Cardiff is a County Borough – one of the select echelon having a Lord Mayor. The city's public services are governed by 75 councillors, and run by the officers and staff of Cardiff County Council, from this stylish headquarters at Atlantic Wharf. As you drive into the city, large signs proudly proclaim that you have arrived in Cardiff, Capital City of Wales – Caerdydd, Prifddinas Cymru. The signs also list Cardiff's twin cities of Nantes (France), Stuttgart (Germany), Hordaland (Norway), Lugansk (Ukraine) and Xiamen (China) – underlining the city's international outlook.

Techniquest

The Techniquest science discovery centre is a year-round, all-weather attraction that provides an entertaining experience for all ages. The highly educational exhibits give you a chance to build a bridge, launch a hot-air balloon, fire a rocket, race an electric car, play a giant keyboard – and much more. The 100-seat Science Theatre hosts amazing shows and demonstrations at weekends and during school holidays. Hands-on sessions in the multi-purpose laboratory teach you about physics, chemistry and the life sciences; the stars and planets appear before your eyes in the Planetarium.

Cardiff Festival

From June to August, Cardiff puts on a sizzling programme of great entertainment around the city and along the waterfront, during the UK's largest free outdoor festival. The staff of Cardiff Council and the Cardiff Harbour Authority are masters of the art of providing a great day out for all the family. Highlights include the Children's Festival in Bute Park, the International Food and Drink Festival, the Welsh Proms at St David's Hall, performances of Shakespeare in the grounds of Cardiff Castle and the Big Weekend of live music at the Civic Centre. Cardiff's far-reaching maritime links are celebrated during the Worldport Festival, which features music from around the globe. Inner-city communities bring the atmosphere of Rio to Cardiff Bay during the annual Carnival. The Cardiff Harbour Festival sees sailing ships, air-sea rescue displays, power-boat races, sailing regattas and musicians bring the waterfront to life.

International Food and Drink Festival

The Singing Chefs are typical of the eclectic mix of musicians and performers who entertain the culinary crowds over the weekend of the Cardiff International Food and Drink Festival. This tasty three-day event is held each July in a tented village at the open-air arena of Roald Dahl's Plass, overlooked by the Wales Millennium Centre. Exhibitors from countries including France, Germany, Norway, Italy, Spain, South Africa and, of course, Wales will introduce you to everything from prime vegetables, meat, fish and delicious cheeses to fine wines, distinctive beers and ciders, liqueurs and luxury chocolates – all of outstanding quality.

Cardiff from the Barrage
The footpath across the
Cardiff Bay Barrage is a
great place from which to
look back at the modern
city and understand why it
grew in this superb
location. The hills in the
distance mark the southern
edge of some 1,000
square miles of coalfield
where, a century ago, a
quarter of a million
miners worked underground.
The sheltered bay was the
obvious place for a seaport
from which to take the coal
out to the world. The bay in
its new guise, following the
construction of the barrage,
is an equally great asset
– attracting new investors,
visitors and residents.

Cardiff Bay Barrage

The waters of Cardiff Bay were impounded by the barrage in November 1999. Its three locks, each 40 metres long, enable visiting craft – and locally based yachts and fishing boats – to pass through. Bascule bridges raise sections of the road across the barrage, enabling vessels with tall masts – including impressive sail-training ships – to visit.

A large fish pass provides a safe route for the migratory salmon and trout of the Taff and Ely rivers. In addition to being the catalyst for the redevelopment of Cardiff Bay, the barrage also alleviates flooding of the low-lying city centre by excluding tidal surges.

Penarth Pier

A century ago, Penarth's solid villas were occupied by Cardiff merchants, shipowners and sea captains. The town still has the charm of a genteel seaside resort and is known as The Garden by the Sea, on account of its attractive parks and public gardens. A stroll along the pier is essential – the paddle steamer Waverley and motor vessel Balmoral call by in summer. If you fancy a longer walk, follow the coastal path from the esplanade, southward for a couple of miles, to Lavernock Point. In spring 1897, Marconi transmitted the first radio messages over water from here – firstly to the island of Flatholm, then to Brean Down near Weston-super-Mare.

Moorings at Penarth Marina

As befits a prominent seaport, Cardiff makes excellent provision for aquatic sports. Penarth Marina, built around the historic Penarth Dock, provides berths for over 300 yachts – along with a boatyard and a restaurant. Two yacht clubs offer membership and facilities. Cardiff Bay Yacht Club, formerly the Penarth Motor Boat and Sailing Club, occupies an impressive clubhouse where the Ely river flows into the bay. Cardiff Yacht Club, near the St David's Hotel, was founded in 1899 by the crews of Bristol Channel Pilot Cutters. It aims to provide fellowship for all who wish to go afloat in anything from large yachts to small dinghies or motor boats, or to go sea angling.

8

Artist's impression main image courtesy of Aspers.

Artist's impressions inset images
© Cardiff International Sports Village 2002.

the future

Cardiff International Sports Village

Construction of the £700 million International Sports Village is in progress on the attractive Ely peninsula in the western part of Cardiff Bay. The project is spearheaded by Cardiff County Council, working in partnership with major developers including retailers, housebuilders, a casino and sport and leisure operators.

There will be state-of-the-art facilities for water, ice and snow sports; high-quality leisure and entertainment venues; a casino and bayside hotel; an attractive range of prestigious homes and a great choice of restaurants, bars and shops. For sports fans and participants, there will be a large indoor arena – which will host major sporting events, including ice-hockey – a 50-metre swimming pool, health and fitness studios, a real snow slope and an ice rink.

Easily accessible by means of the excellent transport links serving Cardiff Bay, the International Sports Village will be a destination of European significance, where the people of Wales and visitors alike may enjoy world-class attractions for all the family.

St David's Centre

The St David's 2 project – a redevelopment of the southern part of the city centre – is based on the latest architectural and planning ideas. A mix of shops, restaurants, bars and apartments will be set around pleasant squares and arcades. The St David's Partnership, which brings together major investors, is the driving force behind the plans to transform the heart of Cardiff. As one of the most important city developments in the UK today, the scheme will build on existing assets, including the St David's Shopping Centre and much of The Hayes. Aiming to secure Cardiff's place as a leading European capital city, and a fitting gateway to Wales, the development will work in harmony with other attractions in and around the city, including the International Sports Village and the Wales Millennium Centre.

Artist's impression courtesy of St David's Partnership Cardiff.

St David's Centre

The St David's Centre will provide John Lewis with its first presence in Wales, in the shape of a 260,000 sq. ft department store. Anchoring the whole development, this store will be designed to complement the existing fabric of the city centre. The Hayes is set to become a European-style boulevard, incorporating three new public squares, and there will be a new and iconic central library. With Cardiff fast becoming a 24-hour city that embraces an emerging café culture and a trend towards city-centre living, St David's 2 will offer apartments, cafés and restaurants situated within a vibrant, pleasant and safe environment. Whilst pedestrianisation is central to the development, improved transport and access are also key aspects. Two new car parks are planned nearby and better public transport will improve access to the city.

Artist's impression of new John Lewis department store with iconic Library Building, courtesy of St David's Partnership Cardiff.

Index of Images

Cardiff Facts and figures

Cardiff was awarded city status by Edward VII in 1905, became capital of Wales in 1955 and a centre of government in 1999, with the opening of the National Assembly for Wales. It is a thriving, energetic hub of commercial and cultural activity.

Although the city was established on the wealth of a vast coal empire, much of the heavy industry has now gone, to be replaced by government establishments and a large service sector made up of a wide range of financial, insurance and banking institutions.

The media industry is also a significant employer. Cardiff is home to broadcasters BBC Wales, ITV Wales and S4C and has a flourishing arts and cultural scene.

It is also a place of research. In 2002, Cardiff University was placed 7th out of 106 universities and colleges in a nationwide analysis of research quality. The value of its research is indicated by a huge growth in investment by industry, commerce and the public sector. Cardiff's proportion of knowledge-based employment is higher than the UK average.

As a consequence of its success, Cardiff is experiencing rapid growth. The official mid-year estimate of the city's population was 315,100 in 2003, a growth of 6.1% since 1991 – compared with 1.9% for Wales as a whole and 3.4% for the UK. A steadily increasing percentage of the population speaks Welsh, one of the oldest languages in Europe, which is thriving through its prominence in education, broadcasting, youth culture and new media.

Cardiff is far from parochial – its rich past as one of the world's busiest seaports has given it one of the oldest multicultural societies in the UK. An estimated 1.3% of the population is black, 3.9% Asian and 1.2% Chinese. More than 30,000 students from all over the world are based in the city.

Cardiff is also enjoying a renewed maritime focus. The development of Cardiff Bay has seen a regeneration project of international significance. The Cardiff Bay Barrage was designed to create a new waterfront environment for the city. The impounded waters of the Taff and Ely rivers now form a huge 200-hectare freshwater lake having an 8-mile waterfront, around which a new generation of government, commercial, residential and leisure developments has grown.

Cardiff is a great place in which to live and work. In 1999 it was the most highly rated city in the Healey and Baker study of the UK's best working cities. It scored highly on location of offices, ease of commuting, cleanliness, parking and shopping facilities.

Source: Cardiff Council

CARDIFF

Population in 2003
315,100

Total households in 2004
135,000

Welsh speakers in 2001
31,950

Climate
The climate varies from mild winters, rarely below freezing, to temperate summers, typically in the 20° to 25° Celsius range.

Twin towns
Stuttgart, Germany, since 1955; Lugansk, Ukraine, since 1959; Nantes, France, since 1963; Xiamen, China, since 1983; Hordaland County, Norway, since 1996.

Tourist attractions
The Assembly at the Pierhead, Cardiff Bay Barrage, Cardiff Castle, Cardiff Visitor Centre, Cardiff Bay Visitor Centre 'The Tube', Castell Coch, City Hall, Llandaff Cathedral, Museum of Welsh Life, St Fagans, National Museum and Gallery, Roath Park, Techniquest.

Major sporting venues
Cardiff Arms Park, Cardiff Athletic Stadium, Cardiff Bay Water Activity Centre, Maindy Cycle Track, Millennium Stadium, National Indoor Athletic Centre, Ninian Park, Sophia Gardens, UWIC Sports & Leisure Club, Wales National Ice Rink, Welsh Institute of Sport.

Theatres and arts venues
Chapter Arts Centre, Llanover Hall Arts Centre, New Theatre, Norwegian Church Cultural Centre, The Old Library, Sherman Theatre, St David's Hall, Wales Millennium Centre.

The Creative Team

Trevor Fishlock

Trevor Fishlock is an author, broadcaster and foreign correspondent. He began his career on The Times as staff correspondent in Wales, later becoming chief correspondent in India and New York, then Moscow bureau chief for The Daily Telegraph. As a roving writer he has reported from more than 70 countries and has been International Reporter of the Year in the British Press Awards. He lives in Cardiff and writes and presents the television series Fishlock's Wild Tracks and Fishlock's Sea Stories for ITV Wales. He has written books about Wales, America, Russia and India. 'Conquerors of Time', his celebration of 150 years of exploration and invention, was nominated for Welsh Book of the Year in 2005.

Pictured from left to right
Steve Benbow, Steve Hall,
David Williams, Peter Gill.

Peter Gill

Peter Gill is a graphic designer who worked in advertising and television in London and Cardiff, before launching the design consultancy Peter Gill & Associates. He has worked on a broad range of projects for clients including the Welsh Rugby Union, National Museums & Galleries of Wales, Welsh Development Agency, Welsh Water, Lake District National Park and the Welsh National Opera. He has won numerous design awards and articles about his work have featured in the design press – visit www.petergill.com – Peter launched Graffeg, the publishing arm of Peter Gill & Associates in 2003.

Steve Hall

Steve Hall is a Senior Graphic Designer with Peter Gill & Associates. A design graduate from Coventry, he has been lead designer on many high-profile projects including the National Assembly Visitor Centre and the Tolpuddle Martyrs exhibition in Dorset. The distinctive style of his work is the result of the creative flair and of his particular interest in photography and typography. He designed the hardback edition of Cardiff – Caerdydd and the associated photographic book Landscape Wales – Tirlun Cymru.

Steve Benbow

PhotolibraryWales, based near Cardiff, was launched in 1999 by Steve Benbow, a respected photojournalist, and his wife Kate, an experienced picture researcher and editor. It represents the work of over 150 photographers and, having over 100,000 original images, is the largest searchable source of contemporary images of Wales. PhotolibraryWales supplies images of the arts, travel, sport, business, lifestyle, personalities, environment and more abstract concepts to publishing, advertising, design and media professionals all over the world – the website www.photolibrarywales.com also has a gallery of prints for sale.

David Williams

David Williams is a writer and photographer specialising in the culture and history of Wales. He wrote the text and supplied images for Landscape Wales – Tirlun Cymru, the companion volume to this book, and is a contributor to PhotolibraryWales. His interest in the history of the sea and ships takes him to spectacular locations around the world as a contributor to publications, exhibitions and television programmes having maritime themes, and as a guest speaker on cruise ships. But he is equally happy working in Wales – where, as he is always quick to point out, the cultural and scenic delights are second to none.

The Photographers and the pages on which their images are shown.

Andrew Davies 61; 112

Andrew Orchard 90; 92

Andrew Hazard 86

Andy Stoyle 96

Billy Stock 28; 32; 37; 44; 49; 58; 66; 81; 84; 98; 100; 102; 110; 114; 120; 122; 126; 134; 135; 136

Brian Woods 48

Ceri Breeze 62; 94

Chris Colclough 38; 39; 79; 104; 128; 129; 130; 131; 146; 147

Chris Stock 74

David Angel 30; 50; 80

Duncan Miller 56; 148

Dave Williams 101

David Williams 33; 68; 116; 123

George Makkas 65

Glenn Edwards 77; 82

Huw Jones 26

Jeff Morgan 60

Jonathan Pimlott 80

Ken Price 148

Les Evans 42

Mark Bradwick 138

Neil Turner 34; 36; 88; 138; 144

PGA 41; 46; 70; 139

Simon Regan 4

Steve Benbow 40; 45; 52; 54; 55; 64; 72; 73; 78; 87; 94; 101; 106; 107; 108; 109; 118; 132; 140

Acknowledgements

Our thanks to: Cardiff Central Library; Cardiff City Football Club; Cardiff Devils Ice Hockey Club; Cardiff County Council – Tom Morgan, Paul Mannings, Hazel Ilett; Cardiff Rugby Club; Glamorgan Records Office; National Museum & Gallery Wales; South Wales Echo; The Western Mail.